# Grieving God's Way

*Lisa,*
*To God Be The Glory.*
*Thank you.*
*Lydia M. Douglas*

By Lydia M. Douglas

P.O. Box 2535
Florissant, Mo 63033

Copyright ©2011 by Lydia M. Douglas
All Rights reserved. No part of this book may be reproduced or transmitted in any forms by any means, electronic, mechanical, photocopy, recording or otherwise, without the consent of the Publisher, except as provided by USA copyright law.

All scriptures are taken from the King James Version of the Bible.

Edited by: Kendra Koger

Edit/Proof Reader: Lynel Johnson-Washington

Cover Designed by Sheldon Mitchell of Majaluk

Manufactured in the United States of America

Library of Congress Control Number: 2011905138

ISBN: 978-0-9834860-0-8

For information regarding discounts for bulk purchases, please contact visit Lydia at www.booksbylydia.com or Prioritybooks.com. You can email the author at: Lydia Douglas ldoug48305@aol.com.

# Grieving God's Way

Published by Prioritybooks Publications

Missouri

# Dedication

I dedicate the words of this book to my late husband, James H. Douglas Sr. and to my three sons, Gerry, Mark, and James Jr. and their wives and my grandchildren. My husband, James, was an important figure in all of our lives. He was the head of our household, the strength and he was like a gentle giant. We miss him greatly.

This book is also dedicated to everyone who has lost a loved one. This includes your spouse, a child or your pet. When you lose someone dear to your heart, you suffer by grieving.

To others whom have impacted my life, I dedicate this book to you also. To my church family at Shalom Church City of Peace, thank you so much for your support. You all have been wonderfully supportive in my time of need.

To Dr. F. James Clark, Pastor and Founder of Shalom Church City of Peace, I thank you for your leadership, support and encouragement.

As I write this book I am reminded of verse, 1 Peter 5:7 that tells us to cast our cares. It reads: "Casting all your care upon him; for he careth for you." I know that God cares for me because He knew what I was going to experience before it even happened. He prepared me for so many things and I am forever grateful for His love and guidance.

I am hoping the words of this book will give you, the reader, hope and endurance to continue on and reach out to help and support others. It is important for each of us to understand that within God's love for us He always has a plan. Sometimes we may not understand it, but if we allow God to continue to work in our hearts and spirits we will find that He never leaves, us even when we experience such great pain and we think we cannot make it. But God is good and He is always with us.

To everyone who has lost a loved one, I dedicate this book to you.

Thank you very much,

Lydia M. Douglas

# Introduction

## **Grief**

Although there are many causes for grief, such as the death of a loved one, the loss of a pet, parents separating or divorcing and even losing something such as a job or a home; death is a major cause of grief for many people. To many of us this loss is so great we sometimes feel as if we cannot make it. It is important to know that grief is a normal reaction to loss and we should not feel bad about expressing our pain.

Grief involves so much pain that involves the heart and so many ranges of emotions that affect our thoughts and actions. We experience sadness, fear, anger and a host of other feelings. There is a time of loneliness. In times like these we must not question God, but place our utmost confidence in Him.

Tragedy must not be blamed on God. We have to accept what has happened. God allowed it to happen for whatever reason. So we have to accept it and move forward and keep pressing toward the mark, which is the high calling of Jesus Christ.

Regardless of how bad we think the circumstances are, God can work redemptively in and through the situation. He knows our pain and when we are obedient, He will bring us through.

We may feel as if we are walking through a very deep and lonely valley, but we cannot look back. We cannot undo the past, if we could, we would. If we stay in His loving arms we can come to a new mountaintop experience of God's grace and His mercy. We must trust the Lord and all of His promises, even though we cannot see them as God sees them, we just have to trust His Word.

We must learn to continually believe God in the midst of any discouragement, and the peace of His Spirit will overcome the loneliness that we may sometimes feel.

God wants us to have His comfort and to walk in His joy and peace. As stated in, 2 Peter 1:2, "Grace and peace be multiplied unto you through the knowledge of God, and of Jesus our Lord."

When you feel too overwhelmed with grief, talk to someone like your minister, this person will be able to help you through listening and counseling you.

# Life Goes On

# Before and After Death

"The man who completed my life was gone. Though I lived many years without him, I was at a loss at how I could live the rest of my life without his presence. My life was suddenly divided into Before and After chapters…"

Since my life was suddenly divided into Before and After chapters, and there was no going back to Before. I realized I had a choice in how I wanted to live the After. I had to decide all by myself.

In order to have a blessed tomorrow, it has to start with the fulfillment of today. The fulfillment starts with giving God all of the praise for what He has done and what He is going to do.

In talking with others who have gone through the same thing, I now realize that my loss is not God's punishment or that God is testing me. I know that God shares the hurt in my heart, and wants to lead me to a new level of hope and peace in Him.

He does know what I am going through. He lost His Son, so yes, He does know we are suffering. But God has promised that He is always with us even to the end. I hold steadfast to God's promises.

*In Matthew 28:20, it reads:* "Teaching them to observe all things whatsoever I have commanded you: and, lo, I am with you always, even unto the end of the world. Amen." I am so glad that I can count on God. He promised to always be with us and that includes when we are happy, sad, or grieving.

## Before Death

My married life started with my husband, James H. Douglas Sr. when we met on the sidewalk of Delmar Street in St Louis, MO. The first time I laid eyes on him, he said, "I am going to marry you." My response was, "I don't think so." I really did not believe that this man I'd just met would be my husband. Well, it did not happen as I thought it would.

I had just come to St Louis from Arkansas and he had just come from Tennessee. I was living with my aunt and he was living with his sister. There was just one house between where we both lived. He would stop by and talk to me every day when he saw me out front on the sidewalk or the porch.

Each time we would talk, I felt closer to him. We dated for a short time and then we got married. At that time you could just go to the court house to get your marriage license and there were always ministers around. They would marry you right there on the spot in a room set aside for the ceremony. I believe that all these years later it is the same way, except judges marry you at the courthouse.

But on our day at the courthouse a minister said he had a wedding room set up in his home where he did weddings. We left the courthouse and went to his domicile. The room was set up beautifully. It had more of a wedding feeling and it made the ceremony very special for us. In addition, his wife played the piano and we marched into the room and he married us.

We did not have a car at the time. We depended on my aunt, who drove us to the minister's home, and after the wedding was over, she drove us back to our apartment. We had gotten an apartment the day before and had bought some furniture. James was a working man. On the day we were married, we returned to our apartment and James changed clothes and rode the bus to work. From the first day of our marriage to the day of his death, James worked very hard. For thirty-nine years he provided for his family.

During our marriage, we raised three sons, Gerry, Mark, and James. We went through some very interesting times. Looking back, it all seems amazing. Three boys! Wow! I was the only female in the house with one bathroom.

In retrospect, our early days were not bad. James and I were both raised with strong morals, values and principles. An old adage says "The apple does not fall too far from the tree." We raised our sons the same way.

When our oldest son started school, I would walk him to school and go back to meet him after the school day was over. We only lived a few blocks from the school he was attending. Eventually my son told me he was a big boy; he knew the way to go and the way to get back home.

Although I trusted him, I wanted to be sure that he was safe. In the morning, I would get him started on his way, and then I would fall back, but still walk blocks behind him, watching until he made it. He did not know I was doing this. I monitored him after school as well. I would stand behind a truck or car, wait on him and when he appeared, I would fall back and follow him. He never saw me.

By the time the middle and the youngest son were ready for kindergarten, we had a car. I would drive them to school and James Jr. would cry all the way until he got in the classroom and then he started to play with the other kids. His brother said he would stop crying as soon as he got into the toy room.

One day, as I was standing around the corner, looking for Gerry, my other two mischievous sons, Mark and James Jr., set the house on fire, looking for candy money. They were using matches as a light to check under the sofa cushion. Still to this day, they each blame the other for starting that fire.

Other than the normal things that happened when the boys were very young, there were no major problems.

\*\*\*\*\*\*\*\*\*\*\*\*\*\*\*\*\*\*\*\*\*\*\*\*

Forging ahead to teen years…

My husband James had great patience. He taught all of us how to drive. He started training the boys at age fourteen. He would allow them to start the car and then turn it off.

At age fifteen, he actually allowed them to drive. At that time, the stores were not opened on Sunday. He would take them to the parking lots and teach them to drive and park in the open spaces. They also went to school lots as well. He needed the large open spaces, so they could really get a good practice in driving a longer distance.

His objective was for them to have experience when they applied to get their licenses and drive on their own. At fifteen, the oldest son had gone to the store and was just a couple of blocks from home when the police pulled him over. He had to park the car and walk home. He did not get a ticket, but he did not drive by himself again until he got his license.

Mark caught on to driving pretty well, but James Jr. did not have the same interest, so it took him a bit longer to learn. He put his bike before the car. Our children were very active. All my sons were involved in sports and we all spent time at various games and Boy Scout meetings.

We paid for them to learn to swim, even though neither

one of us could swim. But we always would go to the pool when we went on vacation. They all got jobs when they became of age, even though Gerry got his first job at fifteen. When they received their pay they would spend $10.00 at the grocery store on hotdogs, buns, bread, milk, etc. They would purchase whatever that ten dollars would buy and they would bring their receipts back to show us what they spent.

Those were just life lessons we were teaching them and it has paid off. We wanted our children to be responsible with their money. James spent a lot of time teaching our children. These little lessons would come in handy as children would mature and leave home. He also taught them how to do things around the house and that has paid off as well. This too was a part of growing up and being responsible.

One of the ways James taught the boys responsibility was by teaching them that if they drove the car, they had to replace the gas they used. This was one big problem my husband had with all three boys. They would drive the car, burn the gas up and forget to replace it. Even though they said they put gas in the car when they left, but driving around the community and who knows where else, they burned that and what was in there as well. James would tell them to fill the tank back up. It was good to have him around to teach the kids responsibility. This too, was a part of growing up and being responsible.

The boys had to cut the grass, take out the trash, clean their rooms and most of all stay in school in order to be good citizens in life. In cutting the grass they would divide the lawn up in three sections, the front, the back, and the side. Of course they all cut differently.

James bought them a snow shovel to tend to the neighbor's snow and a leaf rake, so they could remove leaves and make money. Whatever money they made was theirs to keep. They all have said, "Pops taught us a lot." (Pops is what two of them called James.)

Through it all, they were good kids and had good friends. We both agreed on the same protocol for raising them. They all did well and all graduated. Our oldest son, Gerry, joined the Marines. Not only did I believe he fell in love with the Marines' uniform, but he also wanted to serve. The middle one, Mark, went on to college; James went to college as well and then went into the Army and has done more traveling than any of us. They are all doing very well in life with their families and are very independent.

James was a good father. He and I made a lot of sacrifices, but we made things work for the good of our family. We became each other's best friend and built a trust between the two of us. We all went to church together, went on vacation and family gatherings together. We supported our children in all of their sporting events. We were a family, and we did everything together.

My husband was so proud of all of our sons. James loved our grandkids too. They were so important to him.

He even taught them how to play checkers and shoot pool. The grandkids are being raised pretty much the same way our boys were raised, with morals and values.

God gave us what we needed to raise our kids and become the family that we were. We both worked very hard to get all of them set for life. For that, I am very grateful.

I am so glad that he got to see how and where all of them lived and to see that our work was not in vain. Not only did we teach responsibility in the home, we also taught it in church. We all went to church and we all worked in church as ushers, choir members, Sunday school teachers, youth group organizers and supporters.

After church on Sundays we had dinner together at the dining room table. In order to accomplish this we had to be on the same page with each other, I thank God for that. My husband and I became one to keep our children and our family on the same accord. Raising our sons was hard enough to do together, but separately it would have been much more difficult. We became one, just as God said we would. Matthew 19: 6 states, **"Wherefore they are no more twain, but one flesh. What therefore God hath joined together, let not man put asunder."**

*****************

After thirty-nine years of marriage, and doing everything together, it has been an adjustment for me to do things all by myself. But with the help of God I am still standing, because I am standing and believing in His Word.

Even now when I am in the mall or just looking in stores and see something I like, I have no one to tell me, "That looks good, or you can be my model with that outfit on." James used to say those words to me. Hearing words of encouragement does make a difference. We truly had a wonderful life. We were each other's best friend. We had a trust that was unshakeable.

After the sacrifices we made to get our children set for life, we celebrated each other. God allowed us to have fun and we both enjoyed doing what we did. Just riding around town and looking at houses and stopping to get a soda or an ice cream cone.

We were each other's biggest supporter. As an author, I often had to do book signings, and he was there for me at all times. He would drive me out of town for engagements. He was there for me during every endeavor. Not only was he my supporter, but he was definitely my helpmate.

We would participate in the Breast Cancer Walk together. That was very special, he had cancer in his family and we would walk to contribute and help with the research. We would go to the Cardinals baseball games and have a great time. We would eat hotdogs together at the games, expensive as they were. But who can go to the game and not buy a hotdog?

We would also watch baseball and football games on television together because it was more fun than watching alone. We had our fun and we had it in a good way together. We would go to breakfast, lunch and dinner. But our discussions were who would pay the dinner ticket and who would leave the tip. I won most of the times. Even though my tip was not as much as he would leave, but hey, it was a tip, okay!

We would go to the movies and discuss who would pay for the tickets and/or who would buy the popcorn. I won that most of the time as well. One time, I bought the popcorn and one large soda, yes one soda, but I got two straws….of course he said I cheated. That was the type of relationship we had.

I would always get my clothes out on Saturday night for Sunday and he would peek and see what I was going to wear and then he would match his shirt or tie with what I was wearing. I miss that so much.

James was so much fun to be around. He finally talked me into wearing western boots. I have to admit they are really comfortable and I like wearing them. I also have some matching western hats.

We would go to the park and I would walk and he would ride his bike, he would pass me three or four times. We would always stop and get something to eat before going home. He was looking into taking a class in motorcycle riding when he retired. I told him I was going to keep my feet on the ground until he got it together real good.

We would go downtown to the Riverfront and just walk, meet people and just enjoy each other. We would get something to eat while we were downtown. We had a sense of closeness in our life that no one could tarnish.

We would take a trip on a cruise boat and just enjoy each other. Our church would have black-tie affairs and we would dress up and go to those as well.

We would ride around in new subdivisions and look at homes and wish. God blessed us with our second home. We have three bathrooms, where we had just one when everyone was at home, but we made it with that one bathroom with five people using it.

We went through some hard times in our life, we had no one to teach us how to be married, raise a family, be a homeowner, or hold a job all at the same time at a very young age. We just figured it all out on our own, and with the help of God, it all worked out for our good.

Another reason it worked was the fact that we kept others out of our marriage, relationship and business. Whatever went on in our house stayed in our house and between the two of us.

Our kids did not even know when we were upon hard times. One time the lights got turned off during the summer, so we stayed outside until almost nighttime and then we went in the house when it was time for bed.

Even though we both had jobs, we did not know how to manage money. But everything we went through, we went through it all together. Through it all, we always kept a roof over our heads, and food on the table. Our kids did not know that many times we would go to the resale stores and buy whatever we could use or find. But James and I made it.

James was a hard worker. I would get up at 4:00 in the morning and fix his breakfast and lunch for him to take to work. When he got home after work he would have a hot home-cooked meal for dinner. Sometimes he would call me and tell me that he would be late getting home and I would wait for him and we would eat dinner together.

We enjoyed each other to the fullest. All of the above were the ingredients that made the thirty-nine years of marriage. We talked about renewing our vows. We were going to take a trip and that was going to be our honeymoon that we did not have.

But that did not take place; God said his years on this Earth were up. God was in control and He still is in control. I think of James with gladness not sadness. We had some good times and that left me with good memories.

With all of the good memories we had together, God has kept me standing on His strength. And for that I am grateful.

I was with him when he took his last breath. I was at

the hospital when they pronounced him dead. I told God I was not angry with Him, but I do need His strength to get through this, and He has not failed me yet.

I thank God for the life He allowed us to have and for the good memories of a good marriage.

I tell you about my life with James in this brief, condensed chapter about us because you have to know what I had to understand what I lost. He was the love of my life. I appreciate and love God for giving me the opportunity to experience this kind of love in my time. James was a good man, a great husband and an excellent father. I was blessed to have that kind of commitment and dedication and mostly love in my life. I miss it. I can only thank God for the life He allowed us to have. We loved each other and were the family God oriented. It was a great Before, before I lost the love of my life.

# Life After Death

The word widow, according to Webster Dictionary, means "a woman whose husband has died." When I heard this word widow spoken, it hit me like a rock. I was sitting in church and the minister was delivering her message, she said she was a widow and had been a widow for some time.

I had a light bulb moment. I am a widow. I am a widow. Now at that time, my husband had been gone for about six months. I had not given that a thought as far as myself goes. After three years it is still hard to say and accept.

I will always remember that day. Sunday, September 30, 2007, 10:30 a.m. The death of a spouse is overwhelming. Sometimes life might seem unfair, but you have to accept it and go on. There are many changes that take place when one loses a spouse. One of those changes is that you now have a new title. Am I Mrs. or Ms.? For me, the word "wife" has been replaced with widow. It is a title that is given without choice.

To become widowed is to suffer one of life's most profound losses. When you two had become one in your relationship and one is gone, you actually lose half of you; it takes time to rebuild.

The transition from wife to widow is a very real, painful and personal transition. It is not easy to adjust to being alone, but you have to be real about it, trust God and go on.

With time, God uses our lives to help and teach others about how we are making it through. There is no time limit on bereavement. Each person has his or her own time span.

But through it all, James will always live in my heart. At first it was very hard to go to the cemetery and see my last name on the grave marker, but now it has gotten much better. The time and year of James death was very hard for me, one reason for this is possibly because it came as a surprise. He had a massive heart attack. He was not sick at all, and he was still working, so I had no warning at all.

All of a sudden I felt as if I was in this world all alone. I know I am not, but that was how I felt at the time. Sometimes now, I still feel the same way.

I went on a cruise with some friends, but it was not the same. It was nice, but James was not there. When I got home I had no one to share it with. I'm not used to being alone. I have to tell myself, if you want to go to lunch or dinner, go. If you want to go to a movie, go. Get your popcorn and enjoy the movie. It is truly an adjustment. I feel as if every facet of my life has been turned upside down. I look around in the house and I am alone. I have dreams of family gatherings and friends, I awake and realize that I am really in this house by myself. This brings about sadness, but I ask God for grace and peace and He has been there for me every time.

Being thrust into marital solitude was not expected. James had planned to work two more years and then retire. We had intended to enjoy retirement with trips overseas to Paris and Hawaii, surprising the grandkids at their sports and doing whatever else we wanted to do. He was sixty years old at his death.

I have dreams of him and when I awake and realize that he is not here that brings about sadness. I ask God for grace and peace and He has been there for me every time. Since he has been gone, my life has changed tremendously.

With this great transition I have to get used to doing things by myself now. But with the help of God, I will continue to make it from one day to another. I am learning to live with the reality of the loss of my husband. Each day the intensity of my pain and grief lessens.

It still hurts sometimes when I see couples in the mall or the restaurant and at church, but I am better at it now than I was. Thanks be to God, He is the one who has kept me and I will continue to trust Him.

I am leaning on so many of God's promises. Including this verse: *2 Corinthians 4:16* which reads, **"For which cause we faint not; but though our outward man perish, yet the inward [man] is renewed**

**day by day."**

Many of us fix our eyes on things we can see, which is temporary. But we should fix our eyes on one person that is unseen, that is God, which is eternal.

Our lives must no longer be viewed with a beginning and an end, but truly as being eternal. The eternity of life does not start when we make it into Heaven, but it starts when we accept Christ in our life as our Lord and Savior. He will see us through all of our troubles. He promised never to leave us, nor to forsake us; and on that we can stand firm.

It is hard, but with help from God I will make it and get to the place of where He wants me. I also lean on another promise from *Matthew 11:28 KJV*, it reads, "Come unto me, all ye that labour and are heavy laden, and I will give you rest." This is His promise to us.

When I am looking for comfort and strength I read *2 Corinthians 12:9:* "…**And he said unto me, My grace is sufficient for thee: for my strength is made perfect in weakness. Most gladly therefore will I rather glory in my infirmities, that the power of Christ may rest upon me.**"

When we are in our weakness, His grace and power is there for us.

I also read *Philippians 4:13* in which Paul said: "I can do all things through Christ which strengthens me."

His grace has surely strengthened me to live a life of victory, while allowing me to share His grace and mercy to others that might be going through the same thing. In that way, I can live as an example of His love in everything I do and say.

I am able to go more places now than before. I am open for a rebirth in my life. I have a future worth enduring and I have found a renewed sense of purpose and pleasure in my life. So many doors have been opened for me, so I am going on, with the strength of God. " In *Isaiah 61:3,* He promised: **"To appoint unto them that mourn in Zion, to give unto them beauty for ashes, the oil of joy for mourning, the garment of praise for the spirit of heaviness; that they might be called trees of righteousness, the planting of the LORD, that he might be glorified."**

So on the promises of God, I have put my garment on and I am not going to take it off. God is reaching His people through me and I do not take it for granted. As I am witnessing to God's people I always tell them these are God's Words, not mine. I am just the vessel that He is using to reach His people.

Jesus is our example to the world and I plan to follow His lead to the best of my ability. We all have a task to do; we don't always know what it is, but when that fullness of time comes He will give us what we need to go forth.

He told us in His Word that "I would never leave you

nor forsake you," In *Hebrews 13:5*, it reads: "**Let your conversation be without covetousness; and be content with such things as ye have: for he hath said, I will never leave thee, nor forsake thee.**" **God also promises never to leave us and that He would never give us more than we can bear. There are times when it feels like we are overwhelmed with problems, but we do get through it.**

I have asked Him: "Are you sure I can handle this?" He did not remove it, so I assume the answer is yes. So I can and will handle it.

I have to remind myself from time to time of what He said in His word. When I am having my down moments, He lifts me up and gives me the strength and courage to keep moving forward toward the mark of His high calling.

When He called His servant home, He left me here to reach His people. I want to be found trying to do my very best. Since we had become one, I told the Lord, "When you called your servant home, you actually took half of me, so now put me back on the Potter's Wheel and make me whole again." I am still a work in progress. He is still working on me.

I enjoy reading this verse for confirmation: Job 23:10, "**But he knoweth the way that I take: [when] he hath tried me, I shall come forth as gold.**"

I thank Him for thirty-nine years of marriage, but life

has to go on and it will go on in the name of Jesus. I will not worry about yesterday or tomorrow. Yesterday is gone and tomorrow has not come and it is not promised to any of us.

*********************

As of now, I am still living in the same home we both shared when he passed away the morning of his heart attack. I can truly say that I was with him when he took his last breath.

I told the Lord that I was not upset with His choice to allow death to come upon him, but I asked for His strength to get me through it all. He has not failed me yet. He is truly my strength from day to day.

I like to travel, but it is not the same when half of you is gone. We had truly become one just as He said we would. When I travel I find myself wishing he was sitting beside me, and then I have to pick myself up and remind myself that he is not coming and I have to go on by myself.

I have my family, church family and friends to call on when needed. So when someone is put in my path that has gone through or is going through the loss of a loved one, I can reassure them that God is there for them.

We are blessed when we reach out and bless someone else. When we open our hands to others, God will fill them up again with His blessings.

*I Corinthians 2:9*

**"But as it is written, Eye hath not seen, nor ear heard, neither have entered into the heart of man, the things which God hath prepared for them that love him."**

Everyone has the right to grieve the way that works best for him or her. No one has the right to tell anyone the way they should be grieving. No one knows the relationship that the other one has had. We just need to be there for them.

Recently, I was blessed to take a trip to Paris. He used me in Paris as well. That was truly a blessing for me. The same God we serve here in America is the same one they serve in Paris, France.

It is truly because of Jesus Christ our Lord that I am still standing with my head held high. Wherever I go and whatsoever I do, I represent a loving and trusting God. I must remember God's promise, "Thou shalt increase my greatness, and comfort me on every side." Psalm 71:21

I must also be patient and wait on the Lord for Him to provide all my needs and renew my strength. Isaiah 40:31 reads, "But they that wait upon the Lord shall renew their strength, they shall mount up with wings as eagles, they shall run and not be weary, and they shall walk and not faint."

In my low moments I have to ask the Lord to help me

to wait on Him. He already knows what my tomorrows will be. I have listed this verse that has helped me through my grieving:

Matthew 5:4 "Blessed are they that mourn, for they shall be comforted." He has comforted me many times. I seek His comfort because He knows my heart and my mind, better than I do myself.

No matter what another person is grieving for, job, housing, or the economy, God is here for us all.

**********************

I work with my church and do motivational presentations at schools and with youth groups. This keeps me busy and for that I am thankful. God has placed me in the path of some very important people and I have been able to be a witness for Him.

When God instructs you to do something, you do it. We don't always know where He is going to lead us, but we must follow if we want to be obedient. So many things in our lives happen for a reason. We won't always know why things happen, but when we are hurting as a result, we have to be a witness for others. Especially if what we went through can help someone else. As a result of losing the love of my life and having James and God to prepare me, I am able to help others. Our lives, triumphs, and pain can be a testimony to others. I never expected that losing James would help me to prepare others before they lost someone they love.

To enjoy a good future, I am not going to waste the present by being sad. I am going on with life to the best of my ability. That is what James would have wanted for me.

Although weeping may endure for a night, remember, joy definitely will come in the morning. I believe that we all will experience pain as we move through this thing called life, but along the way we will also experience much joy. Believe that God will prevail and He is not a liar. When He makes promises to us, rest assured you will see the results.

# We Must Take Care of Our Business

I wrote a book titled, Taking Care of Business, because I was impressed by my husband and from my own understanding and experiences to not procrastinate with our life if we should die. As I want to be ready when Jesus returns, I wanted to be ready should James or I die. My book helps to prepare you for the inevitable. It surely helped me when James unexpectedly died.

God had given James a premonition. He had told me several times that he was going to die before me, and of course I said, "You don't know that." But God was in the midst of it all. He told me all of the benefits on his job and everything have worked out just as he told me it would.

He told me he did not want me to be sad, he wanted me to be happy and he did not want me to be alone. Well, that is in the hands of God.

*Habakkuk 2:3* states:

**"For the vision is yet for an appointed time, but at the end it shall speak, and not lie: though it tarry, wait for it; because it will surely come, it will not tarry."**

We don't always know what God has around the corner for us, but we should be eager and ready to do whatever He has in store for us.

When God told me to get the pre-paid burial plan, I said, "Why, we are not going to die, we are not sick." He told me to get the extra insurance on the house, I again asked, "Why?" He said, "Just do it."

I did what God told me to do. When my husband died suddenly I had all of my business filed away in a file cabinet and that really does make a difference. As I think back, in the eyes of God, He saw my husband's death right around the corner. He was looking out for my welfare for this day right now.

To the readers of this book, if you have not gotten your business in order, take some time and get it in order. Tomorrow is not promised to anyone.

Like you, I did not see it that way, but I am so grateful that He saw favor in me to tell me what to do; and I am more grateful that I was obedient to what He told me to do. I have so much to be thankful for. God was looking out for me, and for that I will always be thankful.

Take some time and sit down with your family and get everything in order. Make sure you have a beneficiary on every aspect of your business. Get the pre-paid burial plan, pick out the plot that you want and pay for that as well.

If you have insurance, that's good, but insurance companies do not write that check the next day and the one that is left has to come up with money to pay for a funeral. Plus, the person who survives will need to live too.

Having your business in order will save you money and time in the future, because, without a beneficiary on your business you will end up in Probate Court; and that is time and money wasted. Do not leave these burdens on your family. Your family should not have to ask anyone for help in taking care of your business.

God has reached so many of His people through me and my testimony. Remember, we are just the vessels that He is using.

I was asked the question, "Have you given yourself time to mourn?" My answer was, "No." My God has been so good and kind to me, I do not have to mourn over anything. Through it all, God has kept me and is going to continue to keep me.

I have continued because I have remained with God, like He said in *Psalm 73:28*, which reads: "**But [it is] good for me to draw near to God: I have put my trust in the Lord GOD, that I may declare all thy works.**"

I will stay connected to the Vine, and the Vine is the Lord Jesus Himself. *Matthew 5:16* reminds me of what God expects me to do. He said, "Let your light so shine before men, that they may see your good works, and glorify your Father which is in Heaven."

I am glorifying my Father when I continue to go on with my life and tell others how God has kept me through it all. I have some bad days, like the holidays and special occasions like my birthday, our anniversary, and his birthday. I wear this happy face because I have God on my side and with him I can do anything.

Yet, I realize because of the significance and love I had for my spouse and the many years we spent together, my memories will not end. There were special occasions where we spent much time celebrating, so when these days reappear I will remember them with love and feeling the huge loss of love I once had.

It will take much time to stop grieving the loss of a loved one. I believe that you may never stop grieving. It will become easier, but it will always be there. There is a time to go on and live the life that God has prepared for you to live.

There is no time limit on grief, but we have to keep it real.

Ecclesiastes 3:1-8 states there is a time for everything, and a season for every activity under heaven.

- To every [thing there is] a season, and a time to every purpose under the heaven:
- A time to be born, and a time to die; a time to plant, and a time to pluck up [that which is] planted;
- A time to kill, and a time to heal; a time to break down, and a time to build up;
- A time to weep, and a time to laugh; a time to mourn, and a time to dance;
- A time to cast away stones, and a time to gather stones together; a time to embrace, and a time to refrain from embracing;
- A time to get, and a time to lose; a time to keep, and a time to cast away;
- A time to rend, and a time to sew; a time to keep silence, and a time to speak;
- A time to love, and a time to hate; a time of war, and a time of peace.

So there is a time for us all to fall asleep in the hands of God only to awake to a life of eternity.

Now it is time to learn to redefine ourselves. Learn new things; get involved in fresh and different things like:

- Exercising
- Get out of the house and meet your neighbors
- Get involved in church ministries
- Checking on older neighbors and family members
- Join a prayer group or start one
- Join a book club or start one
- Eat right, do not binge
- Travel, go places you have not been.

Let yourself feel good again.

- Laugh with friends, have fun. Living your life to the fullness of it. Your loved one would want only the best for you.
- Volunteer your experience with others.

Do whatever God places in your heart, do it in the name of God and your loved one. I ask God to only allow me to speak what He would have me to speak.

There are so many things to do and by the time you get back home you are tired and ready to relax.

# Grieving

# Grieving God's Way

Who do we define as a loved one? When you say you lost a loved one, who is that person to you? Could it be a person, an animal, a relative or friend? In talking about the loss of a loved one, this could be your husband, wife, son, daughter, cousin, grandparents, loss of a job, and even a pet. The Scriptures will remind us of the promises of God.

In this section I would like to address several areas that affect our relationships. I will also address the issues of: When hello means good-bye. What happens to me when part of me is gone? More importantly, how do we work through the loss of wholeness? Finally I will discuss: When a marriage dies.

No matter what we all go through, He knows and will be there for us all. I've been a widow for three years now. After being married for thirty-nine years, my husband, best friend, my buddy, and father of our three sons, had a severe heart attack and passed.

I am still in the adjustment stage, but with the help of God, I get through each and every day. These past three years I have depended on the Word of God to get me through from day to day. And in everything I have to do, I put Him first.

I realize that we all grieve differently, but we can help each other along the way. I have realized that talking with others who have not gone through the same crisis does make a difference.

I was talking with one widow and she said she had not been back to the cemetery since her husband died seven years ago. I go anytime I feel lonely or if I am going someplace near the cemetery; I just stop by and say hi. It does not bother me at all.

So we do grieve differently, and we have that right to do whatever we feel like doing. For whatever reason and for however long it takes.

For guidance I read *Romans 8:28*:

"And we know that all things work together for good to them that love the Lord, to them who are called according to His purpose."

We might not see the good right now, but He said it would be for our good. We just have to keep trusting and believing, knowing that He rewards His people who seek after Him.

Waiting is not an easy task all the time. His timing is not our timing. But His timing is always perfect and always with a purpose.

We know this because in Ecclesiastes 3:1 it informs us that everything has a season and a purpose. It reads: "To every [thing there is] a season, and a time to every purpose under the heaven."

There is a season and a reason for everything, so while I am in this season of my life I am going to continue to give God the praise, in the midst of it all, I am still going to praise Him. I open my heart and mind to receive all that He has for me. Sometimes I might be as an eagle, falling down more than once, but I know He is there to pick me up each time. I also know that with the connection with Him, He will allow me to rise higher and embrace the very best He has in store for me.

God has changed the season of my life. With time I am not going to continue to cry over the one who has left me, but I will rejoice over the One who has stayed. That One is Jesus Christ Himself.

For comfort I read *Psalm 3:3*:

But thou, O LORD, [art] a shield for me; my glory, and the lifter up of mine head."

So when we are down, He will lift us up again and again and again if necessary. I depend on that because He promised us that He will lift us up and I trust Him to allow us to stand on His shoulders when we are down.

There are many Bible verses that we can read for finding comfort in God, such as:

*1 Peter 5:7* states:

"Casting all of your cares upon Him, for He careth for you."

*2 Corinthians 1:3-4* He promised us comfort also:

"Blessed [be] God, even the Father of our Lord Jesus Christ, the Father of mercies, and the God of all comfort; [4] Who comforteth us in all our tribulation, that we may be able to comfort them which are in any trouble, by the comfort wherewith we ourselves are comforted of God."

I have truly cast all of my cares on God. All of this is new to me and I have no knowledge of how to deal with it without casting my cares on Him. He has guided me through every phase that I have been through.

*Lamentations 3:32*

"But though he causes grief, yet will he have compassion according to the multitude of his mercies."

God is working with me. Although I have suffered grief and still am grieving, I know He has compassion for me and when the time is right He will heal my pain.

*John 16:20*

"**Verily, verily, I say unto you, that ye shall weep and lament, but the world shall rejoice: and ye shall be sorrowful, but your sorrow shall be turned into joy.**"

When I trust in Him to fulfill His promises I know my grief will turn to joy. God has a plan for my life and I am waiting for Him to show me what it is.

*I Thessalonians 4:13-14*

"But I would not have you to be ignorant, brethren, concerning them which are asleep, that ye sorrow not, even as others which have not hope.

For if we believe that Jesus died and rose again, even so them also which sleep in Jesus will God bring with Him."

Although James and I are no longer together, I know I'll see Him again. For that, I am grateful. James loved God and He believed God died and rose again. Therefore, I believe I will see James when God returns. Other scriptures I have relied on include:

*Philippians 4:4*

"Rejoice in the Lord always, and again I say rejoice."

When he said rejoice, that is what I do, I am not sad or angry. Disappointed? Yes. I can find comfort in God. He said in His word that He would never leave me nor forsake me and that is a great relief and a sense of ease.

When I feel alone, I know I am not alone. He is with me every step of the way.

That is what He meant when He said, "Rejoice in the Lord always," and I will continue to rejoice.

Staying Encouraged

When you are grieving you have to find the strength through God to stay encouraged. You are truly hurting and sometimes you feel alone, but you have to call on Jesus to hold you up. Be encouraged that He will be there for you in your darkest hour.

I marinate on these Bible verses for all my help.

*Jeremiah 49:11*

**"Leave thy fatherless children, I will preserve [them] alive; and let thy widows trust in me."**

When we do our part by trusting, and being faithful, He will prove Himself unto us in many ways. We cannot even wrap our minds around the wondrous things God wants to do in our lives.

*Philippians 4:11*

"Not that I speak in respect of want: for I have learned, in whatsoever state I am, [therewith] to be content."

*Isaiah 61:1-3*

"The Spirit of the Lord GOD [is] upon me; because the LORD hath anointed me to preach good tidings unto the meek; he hath sent me to bind up the brokenhearted, to proclaim liberty to the captives, and the opening of the prison to [them that are] bound;

[2] To proclaim the acceptable year of the LORD, and the day of vengeance of our God; to comfort all that mourn;

³ To appoint unto them that mourn in Zion, to give unto them beauty for ashes, the oil of joy for mourning, the garment of praise for the spirit of heaviness; that they might be called trees of righteousness, the planting of the LORD, that he might be glorified."

When He said put on the garment of praise, in the midst of our heaviness, He did not describe heaviness. Mine is mine and yours is yours, but in the midst of it all, that is what He expects from us, and when we do our part, He will do His part.

*Psalm 23:6* says, "Surely goodness and mercy shall follow me all the days of my life: and I will dwell in the house of the LORD forever."

This verse reminds me that God's grace and His Mercy have followed me all the days of my life. In these last three years it has not only followed me, but it has been by my side, in front of me, leading me, it has been all around me.

That's how I have made it these past three years, with the help of God.

*1 Peter 5:7*: "Casting all your care upon him; for He careth for you."

I have truly cast all of my cares upon Him because He does care for me. That is the only way that I have made it this far. As long as I continue to give God the glory, He will continue to keep His arms of protection around me.

*Proverbs 30:5*

"Every word of God is pure: He is a shield unto them that put their trust in Him."

The Word of God encourages me. I find peace when I read and study His Word.

He has opened so many doors for me to go forth to do His work, which makes me feel that His favor is upon me for some reason. He could have chosen many others to do His work. So I am encouraged, I believe He has something waiting for me around the corner.

And as I walk through those doors, I believe what *Psalm 119*: 105 states, **"Thy word [is] a lamp unto my feet, and a light unto my path."**

*Jeremiah 29:11*

**"For I know the thoughts that I think toward you, saith the LORD, thoughts of peace, and not of evil, to give you an expected end."**

So as long as I stay in His word, His light will lead me wherever I go. As I look back on these past three years, His Light has been the one that has been carrying and leading me, not me myself. His Light has gotten me through these rough times.

I don't know what my tomorrows are, but I know He holds my future. We have to make small beginnings toward reshaping our lives without the ones we loved, and to know that our seeds of hope can and will cultivate into fruitful tomorrows.

Learning to Cope

*Hebrews 13:5 states*: "Let your conversation [be] without covetousness; [and be] content with such things as ye have: for he hath said, I will never leave thee, nor forsake thee."

Yes, I miss my husband a great deal. More than anyone could ever know. I find myself doing things by myself now, which is a great adjustment for me because we did everything together.

But I am learning to cope. I am getting used to going out to dinner or lunch by myself. At first it was hard, but now I go out and eat, and to the movies by myself. I just get my popcorn and soda and go on and watch the movie.

*Psalm 3: 5*

**"I laid me down and slept; I awaked; for the LORD sustained me."**

I go to bed alone and wake up alone. That is still an adjustment, but I am better than I was, because He has not forsaken me.

*Isaiah 41:10*

**"But thou, O LORD, be merciful unto me, and raise me up, that I may requite them."**

If we are feeling lonely and afraid, He is with us and is holding us in His hands.

*Psalm 147:3*

**"He healeth the broken in heart, and bindeth up their wounds."**

My heart is broken, I am not healed as of yet, but I do believe God's Word; if He said He would, then I believe He will.

*Psalm 147:4*

"He telleth the number of the stars; he calleth them all by [their] names."

God knows everything, even the individual stars, and He loves all of His creations. With us being His children, I know that if He cares this way about the stars, then I know He cares strongly for me.

If He can do that, what we go through is very small to Him. He will not allow us to go through anything that He has not gone through. God lost His Son; He knows how it feels to grieve. He understands and stays with us.

God, the Father, sent His one and only Son to this sinful world to die for our sinful selves. He does know what we are going through. We just have to wait on Him to rebuild us again.

*Isaiah 40:31*

"But they that wait upon the Lord shall renew their strength; they shall mount up with wings as eagles; they shall run, and not be weary; and they shall walk and not faint."

That is worth the wait. Oh, how I love Jesus. I know HE loves me.

*Hebrews 10:36*

"We just need to persevere so that when you have done the will of God, you will receive what He has promised."

I believe God will provide for me. He will keep me because I am doing the will of God. I work hard to do this.

*Psalms 18:30*

**"As for God, his way [is] perfect: the word of the LORD is tried: he [is] a buckler to all those that trust in him."**

I can never be as perfect as He is, but I keep praying and asking God to bless me to be like Him.

Each one of the previous verses gives me strength and encouragement. I have taken refuge in Him; I can depend on God when all others let me down. Longtime friends, sometimes we lose them along the way. I don't have a choice, but to put all of my refuge in Him. I rely on all of God's Word. If He said it, I believe it. He has not let me down yet, and I know He will not.

# "Why Me?"

As far as the question of ‚Why Me?, I did not ask why, I told the Lord, "I have accepted what You have allowed to happen, just give me strength to go on."

Jesus told His Disciples in Acts 9:5, **"Who art thou, Lord? And the Lord said, I am Jesus whom thou persecutest: [it is] hard for thee to kick against the pricks."**

When we say they cannot kick against the prick, and we do not accept what God has allowed to happen, then we are kicking against the prick. We are saying to God, "I do not agree with what You allowed to happen." I do not want to be in that position with God.

I find it is better to accept it, rely and depend on Him, to get me through this, and He has done just that and more. So I did not ask God why. I am just depending on His Word to overcome.

When we grieve the way He wants us to, then He will give us the comfort that we need to overcome our hurt. He told me to cast all my cares upon Him and that is what I have done and will continue to do. He has kept His Word, He has given me peace and joy, even when I am having a down moment, He lifts me up and says, "Go on."

# Now I Have Hope

*Psalm 29:11*

"The Lord gives strength to His people and the Lord blesses His people with peace."

So that is where my peace of mind comes from, the Lord Himself. Not anything that I do, only the Lord God Almighty.

*Nehemiah 8:10b*

"The joy of the Lord is your strength."

I truly stand on the strength of God, on Him and Him alone!

*Habakkuk 3:19*

"The Lord God is my strength, and He will make my feet like hinds' feet, and He will make me to walk upon high places…"

As the Charles Albert Tindley hymn goes "I will understand it better by and by," and until that time comes, my hope will be in the hand of God. Not in man, or myself, but in God. He has kept me for these last three years and I do believe that He will and can carry me on. That is where my hope lies, in God and God alone!

*II Chronicles 20:15*

"For the battle is not yours, but God's."

I am so glad that I have God on my side. He will fight all my battles. I am never alone.

*Colossians 2:10*

**"And ye are complete in him, which is the head of all principality and power."**

I am so glad my God has all the power. For with Him I too can say I am strong and powerful.

*Isaiah 66:13*

"As one whom his mother comforted, so will I comfort you…"

That is another promise of God that we can rely on.

*Joshua 1:9*

"Have not I commanded thee? Be strong and of a good courage; be not afraid, neither be thou dismayed: for the Lord thy God is with thee whithersoever thou goest."

I am working hard to be of good courage. I know that if I falter, God will lift me up.

*2 Corinthians 6:10*

"As sorrowful, yet rejoicing."

Although my heart is hurting, I still rejoice in the Lord.

*1 Corinthians 7:39*, "The wife is bound by the law as long as her husband liveth; but if her husband be dead, she is at liberty to be married to whom she will only in the Lord."

Although I lost the man I thought I would love and be with forever, I realize that I can love again. God said that I am at liberty to love again. I pray He will lead me to a new love. Until then I will rely on God to send me someone to love again or to know him if he is in my presence. That's how I Grieve God's Way!

# More Promises of God

There is nothing in our life God does not know about. He knows our hearts and our needs. He realizes we will hurt when we lose a loved one, but HE promises to help us to get over it.

*Psalm 10:14*

"Thou hast seen [it]; for thou beholdest mischief and spite, to requite [it] with thy hand: the poor committeth himself unto thee; thou art the helper of the fatherless."

I am so glad God knew the time and hour he would take James from me. My husband knew something because he was preparing me too. Knowing this, I can go on because of the many conversations we had.

There are many things and experiences God allows us to go through because it was the plan. However, He is so compassionate and loving He still helps us to carry on.

*Lamentations 3: 31, 32*

"But though he cause grief, yet will he have compassion according to the multitude of his mercies."

Though He brings grief, He will show compassion, so great is His unfailing love."

There are times when I have felt so alone. There are days I cry and miss James. Sometimes while I am crying others are filled with joy. I realize as time passes, so will my grief. Eventually, my grief will turn to joy.

*John 16:20*

**"Verily, verily, I say unto you, That ye shall weep and lament, but the world shall rejoice: and ye shall be sorrowful, but your sorrow shall be turned into joy."**

Each of us will experience some type of grief or sorrow in our lives. It is how we handle the grief that will set us apart. The reason we go through trials and pain is because it will guide us back to God. We have to put our faith in Him if we are to overcome.

*1 Peter 1:6, 7*

"Wherein ye greatly rejoice, though now for a season, if need be, ye are in heaviness through manifold temptations:

"That the trial of your faith, being much more precious than of gold that perisheth, though it be tried with fire, might be found unto praise and honour and glory at the appearing of Jesus Christ:"

We can ask God to show us a sign of His will for our life.

*Psalm 86:17*

"Give me a sign of your goodness, that my enemies

may see it and be put to shame, for You, O Lord, have helped me and comforted me."

All of the promises that God has promised will stand forever. He is not a God who will lie. All of His promises will come to pass; our time is not God's time. We just have to wait on Him.

# Victory Is On the Way

*Psalm 34:19*

"Many are the afflictions of the righteous, but God delivers him out of them all."

We all go through seasons of difficulty and challenges in life. One of the enemy's traps is to isolate you and convince you that you won't make it. But God promises to deliver the righteous out of all of their afflictions. We are righteous because of our relationship with God through Jesus Christ. We are righteous simply by having faith in Him, His goodness, and the promises of His Word.

He said in His Word, "Many are the afflictions of the righteous." He did not say the road would be easy; we just have to keep our faith and trust in Him.

If we keep our confidence in Him, He will do just what He has promised us in His Word.

I choose to continue to trust in Him, I believe He is working behind the scenes on my behalf. I know that when I get to that fullness of time, He will be there with all of the blessings that He has promised me; and that will make my life a whole lot easier.

*Isaiah 40:8*

**"The grass withereth, the flower fadeth: but the**

**word of our God shall stand for ever."**

God is an awesome God. If He said it, you can depend on it to happen. No matter what happens from day to day, God's words will always remain true. Never doubt Him or His love for us.

# Poetry for the Grieving Heart

## One Day At A time

Soon the sun will shine again

Soon things will be fine

Until it does, trust God above

And take one day at a time

*Author:*
*Judith Morse*

## **To Those I Love**

When I am gone, just release me,

Let me go…so I can move into my

Afterglow. You mustn't tie me down

With your tears, let's be happy

That we had so many years, I gave you

My love, you can only guess

How much you gave me in happiness.

I thank you for the love you each have

Shown, but now it's time I traveled on alone.

So grieve for me awhile, if grieve

You must, then let your grief be comforted

With trust. It's only for a while that

We must part, so bless the memories within

your heart. And then, when you must

come this way alone, I'll greet you with

a smile and a "WELCOME HOME."

*Author Unknown*

I dedicate this poem to my husband. It is not the entire poem, but the last stanza. It is the part that mirrors my heart. He was certainly the best.

## In Loving Memory

A golden heart stopped beating

Hard working hands put to rest

God broke our hearts

To prove to us

He only takes the best.

*Author unknown*

## A Prayer for You

With a prayer I have asked
The Lord to always be with you

To keep you safe and healthy
Through all that you do

From the darkness of the night
And into the light of day

His constant love will comfort
And surround you I pray

The Lord's blessings onto you
And your family the same

All this I ask for you
In His Holy name.

*Author unknown*

## God's Promise

God did not promise
Days without pain
Laughter without
Sorrow or sun
Without rain.
But God did
Promise strength
For the day
Comfort for the
Tears and a light
For the way.
And for all who
Believe in His
Kingdom of love
He answers their faith
With everlasting love.

*Author unknown*

# More about Grief

There are many causes of grief.

- A friend moving away or dying
- The death of a pet
- Parents divorcing or separating
- A love one who is seriously ill
- Breaking up with a boyfriend or girlfriend
- The death of a spouse

These situations can cause some strong feelings and you should seek guidance from a counselor or a minister to help you.

What to do to help someone who has experienced a loss?

- Help them get back to their daily routine by allowing them to set short-term goals. Encourage them to take steps to complete the goals.

- Encourage them to share their feelings. Anytime people are hurting, communicating their feelings will help them to deal with their loss. If they do not want to talk, just sit by their side. Think about how you would feel with a friend sitting with you in a quiet moment. Sometimes it is better for the person to just sit with a friend or loved one in silence. The person is happy you are near.

- Don't forget about the person after the funeral. Continue to visit. Invite them to visit you for dinner or take the person somewhere. The months ahead will be difficult. The person is still hurting and will need you more in the coming months to help them work through their grief.

- Don't forget holidays, birthdays and anniversaries. These are difficult times for the person left behind.

- Offer to help them. Be specific about your availability.

What is grief?

Grief is a strong, sometimes overwhelming emotion for people, regardless of whether their sadness stems from the loss of a loved one or from a terminal diagnosis they or someone they love has received. Grief is the natural reaction to loss. Grief is both a universal and a personal experience. Individual experiences of grief vary and are influenced by the nature of the loss. (Mayo Clinic)

Grief is definitely a process. When people experience grief they go through many reactions, such as: disbelief, feeling numb, anger, guilt, resentment, fear and extreme sadness or despair. All these reactions are very common.

Grief also can cause physical problems such as headaches, dizziness, tiredness and weight loss or weight gain. If you know someone who is going through any of these changes, talk to them and encourage them to seek help.

As a person who has experienced each of these reactions, I understand what people who are suffering are going through; because I have been there and continue to struggle with many of the same reactions. However, I lean on God for support and I talk about my husband as much as I can. I have great memories about him. God is sustaining me and carrying me through my grief.

# Review

For Your Review

If you are grieving or have experienced grief, please list other feelings you may have had or are still going through. This may help others to identify if a loved one is still grieving.

1. _____
2. _____
3. _____
4. _____
5. _____


Since your loss, how do you feel?

_____
_____
_____
_____
_____
_____
_____
_____
_____

A friend once said to me that she did not know what to

do to help me overcome my grief. What can you do to help someone who has lost a loved one and is grieving?

_____
_____
_____
_____
_____
_____
_____
_____
_____
_____

To move on after the death of my husband I began to do other activities like: going to a movie, walking and joining an exercise center. James would have expected me to enjoy my life and to continue to live. List some other things you can do to move on with your life.

_____
_____
_____
_____

Because of my book, Taking Care of Business, that I wrote to help other families prepare, should they lose a loved one, I have opportunities to share my story everywhere. I talk to people living in nursing homes, church members, school staff, people who attend my book signings, friends and others who have expressed an interest in my story. When I talk about my grief and about losing my best friend, this helps me to handle James' death. As time moves on it becomes easier. Who do you talk to when you are grieving, or if you suddenly lose a loved one?

_____
_____
_____
_____
_____
_____
_____
_____
_____
_____
_____
_____
_____
_____
_____
_____

If people do not get help it can lead to other problems such as:

- Sleeping problems
- Thoughts of suicide
- Unnecessary risk taking
- Alcohol or drugs

Be alert if you notice that your loved one is experiencing any of these reactions and seek professional help for that person.

Every day I am learning to move away from my grief. I even include James in some of my activities. If I go somewhere we used to go together, I talk to him and ask him if he remembers this place. I reminisce. I visit the cemetery. I look at our pictures and leave them out for others to see. I even talk about him in my presentations.

What are some other things you can do to create a ritual to help someone or to do just for yourself?

_____
_____
_____
_____
_____
_____
_____

Ways You Can Take Care of Yourself

There are many things you can do to help yourself while grieving. As a writer and author, I find that journaling helps me. It helps me to release my pent-up pain. I can write what I am feeling and not worry about spelling and grammar issues, or even who is reading it. This is for me only. No one will read my journal, at least unless I invite them to. Find a journal you can write in or if you prefer to, type on a computer.

Eat a good diet. I am watching my weight and eating foods that are good for me. I eat plenty of fruit and vegetables. This helps me to feel my best. Staying healthy helps me to feel physically and mentally better.

I also get a lot of rest. I go to bed early and rise early. For many years I did this with James. I would get up early and fix his breakfast and prepare his lunch. I am used to doing this since I did it before. It is a good habit to have.

Finally, I manage my stress by exercising. I take walks through the neighborhood or walk in the mall. I also have joined a fitness center where I go work out at least three days a week. This helps to manage stress and helps me to relax. It is my time for me. I also set aside quiet time for me to meditate and read the Bible.

What would you suggest for someone who is grieving to do to relax?

What do you do to relax?

Know When to Seek Help

Prayer changes things. There is nothing we can do without God and His help is sufficient. However, if you are suffering and grieving and things do not feel better, please know when to get help. For example, if you are:

- Engaged in risky behavior like sleeping with many men or driving recklessly
- Excessive drinking or using drugs
- Arguing and causing problems with friends, relatives, your job
- Depressed for long periods of time
- Feeling overwhelmed with grief and sorrow
- Need to talk to someone
- Physical pain such as sleep problems, headaches, or dizziness

If you feel any of these things, talk to someone you feel you can trust. This could be:

- A teacher
- A minister
- Spiritual leader
- Social worker
- Counselor
- Friend

There are also many organizations that will help too. Please look on the Internet for resources. If you live in St. Louis, Missouri, please dial 211 or 911 for help. Telephone books usually have the most updated information. I have also listed several national organizations to help.

# Resources

# Resources

For help and more information, please contact:

National Hospice and Palliative Care Organization
1-800-658-8898

www.nmha.org

National Mental Health Association
1-800-969-NMHA (6642)

www.nhpco.org

The Dougy Center
1-866-775-5683

www.dougy.org

There are some experts listed below. For additional information, on grieving, research the Internet. There is good information to share with people even before they suffer a loss and grieve. There are many written materials available for your review.

The Journey Through Grief: The Mourner's Six Reconciliation Needs, by Alan D. Wolfelt, PhD

Helping Yourself Heal When Someone Dies, by Alan D. Wolfelt, PhD

A Mourner's Bill of Rights, by Alan D. Wolfelt, PhD
http://www.mayoclinic.org/contact/

If you are interested in teaching a class to provide information, the topics listed below maybe helpful. To help people who are grieving, we came up with a course. You may want to use this as a model or maybe for research.

## Grieving God's Way

Grieving God's Way is a course that aims to offer hope in the midst of our afflictions, providing Jesus Christ as a remedy to the grieving process. The course's principle scripture is 1 Peter 5:7 (Cast all your anxiety on Him because He cares for you.)

- Some sample topics are:
- What is grief? Define it!
- Why me?
- Helping people get over grief
- What it means to grieve?
- Working through grief
- Identifying how you grieve
- Steps to Recovery

# Last Words

Grieving is a normal process. When I lost my husband, I realized this was the lowest and saddest time of my life. Though we may face trouble and find ourselves in situations and unknown positions, sadness and pain, we have to remember that God is still in control and He has not left us alone. If you stay your mind and heart on Jesus, He will help you to overcome the deep hurt you are going through. I know for me God has been and is my strength and comfort. Remember God is with us in all of our sorrows.

My flesh and my heart faileth: [but] God [is] the strength of my heart, and my portion forever.

*Psalm 73:26*

The LORD upholdeth all that fall, and raiseth up all [those that be] bowed down.

*Psalm 145:14*

The LORD also will be a refuge for the oppressed, a refuge in times of trouble.

*Psalm 9:9*

At one time I did not know what to do with my life. I did not know what direction I should be going in. I was not accustomed to being alone. My husband did all of the things around the house considered manly. For instance, he took care of the cars, mowed the lawn, and made repairs on the home and anything else that needed to be done. Those were the things I never had to worry about until he died.

I sought the LORD, and he heard me, and delivered me from all my fears.

*Psalm 34:4*

Cause me to hear thy loving kindness in the morning; for in thee do I trust: cause me to know the way wherein I should walk; for I lift up my soul unto thee.

*Psalm 143:8*

Let not your heart be troubled: ye believe in God, believe also in me.

*John 14:1*

And he said unto me, My grace is sufficient for thee: for my strength is made perfect in weakness. Most gladly therefore will I rather glory in my infirmities, that the power of Christ may rest upon me.

*2 Corinthians 12:9*

Thou compassest my path and my lying down, and art acquainted [with] all my ways.

*Psalm 139:3*

When we need help in determining our new path or direction in our lives, we may not want to tell family or friends but we can trust God. He will not share it with anyone. He cares about us, our pain and disappointments. He will answer our prayers and fill our hearts with joy again.

For I know the thoughts that I think toward you, saith the LORD, thoughts of peace, and not of evil, to give you an expected end.

*Jeremiah 29:11*

Many times along the way, the path becomes dark, lonely and obscure. We might not have an earthly body to depend on but we have a Spiritual body to believe and depend on at all times, and that is Jesus Christ Himself.

And the LORD shall guide thee continually, and satisfy thy soul in drought, and make fat thy bones: and thou shalt be like a watered garden, and like a spring of water, whose waters fail not.

*Isaiah 58:11*

Since God is our provider, we can be assured that He is in control of every aspect of our lives. He will prepare the way before us. If we stay connected to Him, He will never leave us nor forsake us. When we feel as if we cannot go any further by ourselves, all we have to do is look down in the sand and we will see only one set of footprints and we know they are not ours. Those footprints are of God.

## Footprints

When I felt lost and filled with pain,
Falling on my knees to pray, I had to explain.
How my heart ached, losing my soul mate,
I knew Lord You would help me the pain to eliminate.

You picked me up when I was down,
And planted my feet back on solid ground.
I thank You Lord for blessing me,
Even though I lost someone special to me.

When I had no strength to carry on,
You took my hand like a newborn.
I made it through this heartbreak and pain,
I know whatever I go through,
You will be there again.

There was one footprint in the sand,
Because you picked me up,
and kept me close at hand.

I love you for carrying me through a lion's den.
For that I can say Thank You God and Amen.

*Written by Rmjackson*

# Notes

# Notes

# Notes

# Notes

# Notes

# Notes

# Notes

# Notes

# Notes

# Notes

# Notes

# Notes

# Notes

# Notes

# Notes

# Other Books by Lydia M. Douglas

## Stepping Stones to Success

## Reaching Higher Heights

## Taking Care of Business

# My Family

CPSIA information can be obtained
at www.ICGtesting.com
Printed in the USA
FFOW03n0623190318
45704021-46559FF